About the author

What can I say in a hundred and fifty words about myself? If you had three hours I would probably not have said enough.

I was born into trauma literally into a car accident and the start of a difficult relationship with my parents, I have only come to understand in recent times the impact this has had on myself.

I am a mother of three and have been married since the age of twenty-one and my partner is my rock.

When my youngest was six months old I was diagnosed with ME/chronic fatigue syndrome and that was over twenty-five years ago. Along the years I have learned to take life day by day but it has not been easy.

This is a work of fiction. Names, characters, businesses, places, events and incidents are either the products of the author's imagination or used in a fictitious manner. Any resemblance to actual persons, living or dead, or actual events is purely coincidental.

FIFTY DAYS OF POEMS

TRISHA DOHERTY

FIFTY DAYS OF POEMS

Vanguard Press

VANGUARD PAPERBACK

© Copyright 2022
Trisha Doherty

The right of Trisha Doherty to be identified as author of this work has been asserted by her in accordance with the Copyright, Designs and Patents Act 1988.

All Rights Reserved

No reproduction, copy or transmission of this publication may be made without written permission.
No paragraph of this publication may be reproduced, copied or transmitted save with the written permission of the publisher, or in accordance with the provisions of the Copyright Act 1956 (as amended).

Any person who commits any unauthorised act in relation to this publication may be liable to criminal prosecution and civil claims for damages.

A CIP catalogue record for this title is available from the British Library.

ISBN 978 1 80016 515 1

Vanguard Press is an imprint of
Pegasus Elliot Mackenzie Publishers Ltd.
www.pegasuspublishers.com

First Published in 2022

Vanguard Press
Sheraton House Castle Park
Cambridge England

Printed & Bound in Great Britain

Dedication

Dedicated to my loving partner, JD, who is always there to pick me up.
Dedicated to my three loving children who are always with me in mind and spirit.

Acknowledgements

To my dear partner, JD, as without you this book would not have come to life.

Day 1 — The Darkness

Even with the light outside
The darkness swirls in my head
Emotional starkness that cannot be quashed
Distractions come and go, but the darkness lingers
Easy to fall down the deep abyss and never climb out
Courage to accept what I cannot control
The tiresome effort to keep moving forward
Moving each day a little more out of the darkness
To accept oneself with all the scars
Keep moving forward for your shadow matters.

Day 2 — Springtime

The warm hug of sunshine
The gentle touch of a breeze
The sprouting of new growth
A season full of new hopes, new promises
The grey days are but a memory
Positivity ensues on that first sun filled spring eve
Love, laughter and all things new
This is springtime

Day 3 — Soul Mates

He wakes her up from deep slumber
He sees the pill bottle and alcohol beside her
He asks himself why aren't I enough
With his sinking heart he brings her coffee one of her favourite things and he sits silently on the bed, no questions, no judgement
She has so much guilt and asks herself why isn't he enough
Though they share love, they are bound by so much more
They are bound by heartache and secrets
No matter what happens they are soul mates to the end
They are bound forevermore with the love that is theirs
                              alone

Day 4 — Home

What is a home?
Is it a place you've lived in for a lifetime or six months
Is it the people who share your dwelling
What if you are alone under your roof?
Is it the pictures you hang on the wall or the nuances of your personality that make it a home
Is home a one-bedroom apartment or a mansion full of empty rooms
What if your home is in the streets, is it less of a home
Home is where love shines and those around you make you feel welcome
Home is where you fit in that has no definition
      Your home is where your heart is full

Day 5 — Memory

A memory triggered by a smell
A memory triggered by a sound
Is it happy, is it sad
Does the memory linger when the music stops
Years go by and more memories are created
Which ones stand out
Which do we try to forget, can we forget
How long can we hold onto those days gone by that give us hope or inspire us into the next day
Memories are but like butterflies fleeting in the wind
And all shape who we are
   So hold on tight to those memories of a life gone by

Day 6 — Scars

A scar is a story of what has been not what is to be
It is a memory not a stigma
A scar tells of adventures good and bad
A scar no matter its source does not have to define you
A scar can burn into your soul if you let it
Or it can fade into years gone by
A scar can shape us, heal us
A scar can remind us of our story but does not have to stain us
A scar can be a mark of courage
A scar is as individual as your fingerprint
It is a footprint on your heart
Never let a scar damage who you are
                Your story is still unfolding

Day 7 — Time Piece

Why do I wear a time piece?
Where does time begin and
Where does time stand still?
The clock starts our day
Tick Tock Tick Tock
Why do we need the clock ticking on our wall
The sun rises.
The sun sets are not enough to drench our souls
The time piece on our wrist causes us to be hasty
Move without thought
My time piece tells me I'm late
I'm always late
Nature moves slowly with everything in its natural place
The sun and moon guiding all below them
Time is precious be thoughtful with it
   Time cannot be replaced so treasure it

Day 8 — Christina

Oh, Christina where are you now
With your dresses and heels
Your hair magnificent
You would light up the room
Christina your burly voice took me by surprise
I was only a young thing then
I would see the adults whispering in the room
I wasn't afraid of your difference
Christina, you took on the world when the world wasn't ready for you
You were asked to put on pants and a jacket
But Christina you couldn't change who you were
You taught me kindness without realising
You taught me to embrace difference
Where are you now Christina
You were one of a kind
In a world that was judgemental, you stood out like a beacon
You embraced love and showed others the way
Oh Christina, I will always remember you
I will remember your brightness for all my days
Oh Christina, where are you now

Day 9 — Sand and Sea

Sand and sea where I long to be
The sun on my face
The water splashing through to my bones
Feeling nurtured by the blue water beneath me
It's my childhood
It's my adulthood
It's where I long to be, to be in the sand and sea
On these long warm days soaking up the sun
Watching the sun fade into tomorrow
Looking into the ocean blue no care in the world
Sitting on the sand watching the world go by
      The sand and sea no better place to be

Day 10 — Buzz

Buzz buzz buzz
In my head
In the day
Throughout the night
Buzz buzz buzz
Never stops
Thoughts and more thoughts
The buzzing doesn't stop
Over thinking
Planning
Preparing
Holding it all in
Distractions get in the way
Where are my keys
Where is my wallet
Buzz buzz buzz
Try to organise my thoughts
Try to switch off
Headaches
Migraines slowly form
Be still my thoughts
My world will not crack if I can calm the storm that is in my head
Buzz buzz buzz

It's night time now the buzzing needs to stop
Bring on thoughts of calm waters
Bring peace through the night
Pray to keep the buzzing at bay

Day 11 — Dance

Sway to the rhythm
Let it take you to another world
The beat of your heart tunes in
Your feet start to move
The dance speaks through your soul
Your instinct in that moment is to let the music invade you
Your eyes brighten with every drum beat, for in that moment you are transformed
You are one with the rhythm
Don't stop dancing
Be the star for all to see
Nothing else exists but the rhythm of your soul
It's your turn to dance
Do it fiercely
Do it with passion
Don't ever let the beat stop
Keep swaying until your body aches
Keep your heart at one with the rhythm, for as long as you can
Even when you are weary let the music take you to that escape
Let the dance bring tears to your eyes
A smile to your face

Let the rhythm sway you while your eyes are bright
but your bones are weary
Keep your rhythm throughout the night
Let the music guide you to that magical place
Keep on dancing into the sunset
Let the rhythm gently sway you one last time,
just one more time.

Day 12 — First Born

To my eldest,
My first born
You were asked to take on so much so young
You didn't complain
You just battled on
We don't always connect and that is okay
If I call you, you come
You sat by my side while your grandad took his last breath
You are strong, but kind
My eldest the extra burden was accepted
You are my shining star
Your heart is gold
Your soul is full of brightness
Your warmth shines through
My eldest I tried, but I know I wasn't like the other mums
I wanted to give you a fairy princess life but that wasn't to be
To my eldest you always made the best of what was
I could not be any prouder of the person you are
Keep being you for all time and forevermore
                    Love Mum

Day 13 — Tomorrow

Morning bright
Sun shines through your window
Birds sing in harmony
New day new beginnings
What will the adventures be today?
Creating a work of art
An adventure in nature
New day brings new hope,
New stories to tell
Mornings spark something in us
Do something brave
Try something new
Let the bright morning take you to experience new things
Tomorrow morning watch the sunrise and sing with the birds
                Embrace the sunshine

Day 14 — My Son

To my son your stubbornness
Shone through,
The day you were born
No one was going to set you rules to follow
You set life on your terms
The hospital visits never slowed you down
Your resilience is a beacon
Your fierce opinion is no battleground
You underestimate your smarts
Your bull headedness for truth knows no bounds
Your heart's warmth is felt by all who touch you
Your kindness subtle
Your loyalty steadfast
I am proud to call you my son
      Love Mum

Day 15 — My Youngest

To my youngest you danced to your own tune since you could walk
You were always determined to prove everyone wrong
You are strong in will
You don't accept knock backs
You give strength to others in being open about your struggles
You are cautious whom you let into your world
Your creativity sparkles
There is organisation in your chaos
You give without compromise
Your eyes are bright and your heart is willing
You don't take no for an answer
Embrace your individualism for always
                        Love Mum

Day 16 — Family

Family is a conundrum and has many forms
Are they people you grew up with that gave you strength when needed
Are they your community that you've poured your heart into
Is it someone you only talk to once a year, but is as familiar as yesterday
Are family those that share your heritage and history
What about those that stand by you no matter what
Or make you laugh with little effort
Family is whom you let into your tiny world
Share your most treasured thoughts with
Have adventures with
Family is unquestionable love
    May you find your unique family in this world

Day 17 — Sadness

The sadness sweeps in again like an ocean wave
I try to re-focus
The sadness lingers
What have I done
Why did I do that
I can't let the sunshine in today
I'll watch re-runs of my favourite shows
Listen to my familiar sounds, until I can drown the sadness away
There is a new challenge today
I'm supposed to be excited
I'm just anxious
Get up, get dressed, so many decisions
The sadness creeps over me
Like a vine strangling my thoughts
I know I've done some things right
Just need to look into my offspring's eyes to see
Today it's not enough
Tears roll out
I've been here before
I'll be here again
Just hold off the sadness long enough to change the tune in my head
May you find peace away from the sadness
If only for a moment

Day 18 — Pain

The pain, the relentless pain
No words can describe
The inability to speak
The muddle in your brain
From head to toe the pain burns
A bath or two helps for a short while
Weightless calming soak, calms the aching bones
When will it stop
A Panadol or two I know it won't help but I will try anyway
Will the pain ever stop
Morning noon and night
You walk past me in the street expecting me to smile
I'm just trying to put one foot in front of the other
I'm just trying to focus
I ask for the pain to subside for one day
For one night
Head is pounding
Heart is thumping
The pain is indiscriminate
        Just one day to breathe is all I ask

Day 19 — Bullies

Bullied in the classroom
Bullied in the playground
Nowhere to run, nowhere to hide
Has the name calling stopped
I still hear the whispers what did I do today?
Go home I'm getting yelled at
No peace no quiet
I'm so confused always doing the wrong thing
Today they want to fight me
I just want to sit in the classroom
Read a book
Imagine myself in fairy land
The bell's gone, into the music room I go
Feeling safe
Play the clarinet
Escape the torment for a short while
My peers think I'm weird
I get laughed at
I get corrected
My family laughs at me, corrects me
No escape
No one will listen
Bullies everywhere I go and now they live in my head
The torment never leaves

It is grieved for ever after
Life filled with confusion
Life uncertain
No confidence
The bullies stay put in my head
Agatha Christie will shut them up if only for a little while
The bullies follow me wherever I go
Bullies it's time for you to go

Day 20 — Hairdressers

Sitting at the hairdressers
Chit Chat Chit Chat
The familiar chemical smell that stays with you
The stranger that becomes familiar while they wash your hair
Chit Chat Chit Chat
Oh wow I probably said too much
The music plays, you tap away
Waiting for the timer to go off
Tick Tock
Scissors clicking in your ear
Keep your head straight
Don't say too much
Chit Chat Chit Chat
Let them wash, let them cut
Busy in the salon
Patience and calm it has focus
It is familiar, it is comfort
Chit Chat Chit Chat
Feeling fabulous walking away from the hairdressers

Day 21 — Parenting

There is no parenting off button
Children now adults
I want to wrap them up
Keep them away from the darkness that lurks
Stop the pain
Be their comfort
Unconditional love knows no bounds
The adventures when they were young
Providing guidance along the way
You are a parent for all time
Reach out to them before they jump in the water
All at once they will leave
You are still a parent
Their stronghold
Wanting to wrap them in cotton wool to protect them
They are grown
There is no off button for a parent
So pray in silence that you have prepared them
Let your children make their own way
Be a phone call away
You will always be their parent
You will always be their guiding light

Day 22 — Secrets

Secrets here secrets there
Whispers in the corner
Why am I drawn in
Don't tell
It's hush hush, no one can know
Compelling
The burden weighs heavy
Who will keep my confidence
Who can I trust
I'm exhausted
Keep it in keep it secret
When will I be relieved
When will it be okay to tell
Secrets and more secrets
Eating into my life force
Don't smile don't give it away
Hold it all in
Secrets good, secrets bad
All locked in my head
I'll keep your secret safe

Day 23 — Melbourne

Melbourne my birth place
My home,
Littered with markets and alley ways
Wholesome goodness on your doorstep
Beaches in another direction
To delight your senses
Melbourne full of surprises
Influences from around the world
A coffee on every street corner
Your present for the tourists
You have so much to offer the locals
Pubs, high tea and so much more
The city I love
No matter where I go, nothing compares to my home

Day 24 — Clouds

Look up into the sky
I see a cloud a soft fluffy cloud
I want to reach it
It takes on so many forms
We muse as to what shape it holds today
Is it as soft as it looks
Could you jump on it for a moment
Looks like a giant marshmallow
If only I could sit on one
Would it be like a magic carpet
It is out of reach
Out of touch
Piques our imagination on a blue sky day
What shapes will form in the cloud today
Whimsy in the clouds
Dare to imagine sitting on a cloud

Day 25 — Animals

The love from an animal has no words
It is given without question
I am humbled by the animals that have lived in my home
They curl up next to me
They wag their tails
They purr
There is nothing more rewarding than an animal's acceptance of you
Their trust that you will take care of them
Their unrivalled faith in you
This love knows no bounds
It is a gift to be unwrapped daily
We grieve when our animal departs
They crawled into our hearts
Made us smile
They gave us stories
They helped us without knowing
There is no love to compare
When an animal lets you in there is no end
An animal's love is enduring
It hurts to say goodbye

Day 26 — Waiting

Waiting waiting
Patiently waiting
In a queue
In a doctor's office
Waiting for a phone call
Why is it taking so long
Scenarios start taking place
I'm not good enough
Why is patience a virtue
Waiting waiting
For the concert to start
The movie to be released
So much waiting
My head aches trying to stem the flooding of anxiety
No need to honk your horn, the light just changed
No life is worth the rush
What will be will be
A little waiting won't hurt too much
A little patience is good for the soul

Day 27 — Photos

Photos tell a story
A stillness in time
Does it bring a smile
Does it bring a tear
What adventures are told
Photos are markers of time
A memory to reflect on
Who, where
Age stands still in your photo frame
Short reminders of our ongoing journey
Good and bad they serve to remind us
Photos on my walls
Photos in my books
Memories on hold
More stories to be told
Take more photos for the stories to be told

Day 28 — Morning

It's morning I need to get up
Why do I need to get up
Why do I need to get dressed
I'm exhausted
Another night of restless sleep
The sun is shining, time to get up
Put the kettle on
Will a coffee help
Why is it so hard to climb out of bed
My energy depleted
The sun is shining, I try to go outside
To bathe in the sun
I'm still in bed
My body argues within itself
The arguing gets louder
I get out of bed
Will I go somewhere
Will I watch TV
Be productive I try
The energy I had is gone
Getting out of bed is exhausting
I will try again tomorrow

Day 29 — Travel

Planes and trains
Where will I go today
What new places will I explore
What cultures will I embrace
A new adventure
New people to meet
New stories to tell
Sitting on the beach, drinking cocktails
Walking through the jungle
Eating new foods
Get a plane
Get a train
Or take a cruise
Explore in your own backyard
So much to do
So much to see
How did that come to be
What will your adventure be

Day 30 — Phone Call

I say I will try harder
I will try to communicate
You want me to call
I hate using the phone
I call you
You're at work or with friends
Too busy
I'll try again
I go back to old habits put off
Too scared to call
Am I interrupting, I feel like it
When is it a good time to talk
Can we talk, I'd like to
Then I don't know what to say
Are you happy, are you okay
Sometimes I'm unsure of what to say, what to ask
I don't want to say the wrong thing
And then I talk too much
I don't know what to do
I need to figure this out
Just give me time
I need to find my rhythm
I will be brave
I will try again tomorrow

Day 31 — Escapism

Myths, legends, fantasy
They engage us
Spirit us away
Escapism from our reality
Exploration into a new world
It captures our imagination
What are the possibilities
Is it good
Is it bad
Is it fantasy
Is it history
Reading a book
Watching a move
It engrosses us
It gives us insight to what might be
Who doesn't want to fly
Wouldn't it be nice to be invisible
Be your own hero
Possibilities are endless
Our imagination is a river flowing in all directions
What captures yours
Comics, cartoons, immortality
Stories implanted take flight
Where will you be transported

Day 32 — Seasons

Seasons changing
Sun slowly fading
Cooler days are coming
Leaves are falling
Warmer clothes start shining
We look to the warmth of the sun
The singing of the birds
Picnics in the park
Anticipate the blue skies
And the sun fades again
What do we do in the rain
Keep the clouds in the sky not in our head
Playing in the snow, don't let it reach your bones
Shivering by the fire
Have a glass of whisky to warm you up
The sun will shine again

Day 33 — Anxiety

Sitting in the room
Is my hair okay, I struggle to get it just right
You smile at me but I don't know why
Is there something strange about the way I look
What about my clothes
I feel so clumsy
So unsure
Don't want to go out today
I judge myself
I feel you judging me
Am I misreading your intentions
Maybe you're just being nice
I don't know
You don't like my shoes
I don't like myself
I need to accept me before I can accept you
Oh no, I have too much make up on
Maybe not enough
I don't like my hair today
Why do I fuss
I just need to be me
Open the door and take a step
Be bold accept yourself

Day 34 — Cats

The purr of a cat
Nothing more calming
Nothing more relaxing
A cat on my lap
Curled up
Stretched out
Reaching out
Tap tap tap on your hand
Scratch me here, scratch me there
Those big eyes staring into yours
Asking for your attention
Softly manoeuvring next to you
Affection unrequited, just a pat here and there
Trust unguarded
Grateful to be their guardian
Feeling blessed with a purr

Day 35 — Laughing

Laughing laughing
Sometimes no words needed
Just a look
You're in sync with the funny side
Tears roll down your face
Once you start you can't stop
Is it a joke
Is it a memory
Is it a word
Laughing laughing
In time with the one who gets you
Humour the bright side
A movie
A show
Laughing laughing
Tall tales
Past stories
Laughter ensues
You're encapsulated you can't escape
Keep the laughter coming

Day 36 — Love

Love takes on different forms
Happiness
Sadness
Do anything for kind of love
Once you find it, don't let go
Hang onto it tightly
You can't imagine life without it
Love changes with time
Becomes companionship
Complements friendship
Can last a lifetime
Can last a short time
Accepting someone for who they truly are
Love is manic
Is patient
Love is kind
Love is understanding
Standing by through struggles
Brining a cup of coffee when words are a struggle
Love knows no bounds
Love makes you smile
Love makes you cry
Love gives you joy
Love is new beginnings

Day 37 — Nature

Trees swaying in the breeze
Birds singing
The dam invites the wildlife
I'm perched on my swing
Taking in the surrounds
Breathe in
Breathe out
Nature engulfs me
I ponder my thoughts
Peace surrounds me
Beating of the tree, takes hold
The touch of the sun guides me
Plants budding
Let nature take hold
Give into it just for a moment
Let peace restore your soul

Day 38 — Baking

The flour
The butter
What will come to be
Chocolate cake
Treacle scones
Childhood memories stem from the smell
Creativity comes alive
Flavours
Spices
Your senses come alive
Healthy or indulgent
The mood takes you there
Instinctive or measured
Flour and more flour
Not enough butter
Will it come to life
Will it taste as good as it smells
Creams and frosting to finish
The cup cakes are a delight
The scones are a hit
Baking enlightens me
Teaches me patience
Smell infuses the house
And now to taste

Day 39 — Sleep

Sleep doesn't come
The anxiety sweeps over me
The worry of uncertainty
Tomorrow or next week
Or next year, why am I thinking about what ifs
Feeling numb
My skin feels like it's burning
Am I on fire
I toss, I turn
I count my breaths
Still sleep doesn't come
I try to calm my inner storm
Sleep stays away, taunting me
Teasing me, within reach but not achievable
I pray I get to sleep tonight

Day 40 — Anniversary

Another anniversary is upon us
The tides have been rough
The sunsets have been sweet
We could have given up
But we carried on
You were weighted with burdens beyond understanding
You took time to understand
Your patience has been indelible
Risks were taken
Tragedy ensued
But we got through
Adventures and laughter have prevailed
Tough times have been tackled
Our travels of life are not for the faint hearted
We have not crumbled
We have not faded into the abyss
We take life as it comes
We talk
We shout
We pout
But we come back to each other
No better person could I share this life with
Your kindness will stand true

Your hands are calming waters upon my shoulders
My soulmate
My husband
With love

Day 41 — Peter Pan

Can I be Peter Pan for one day
No cares in the world
Playing with the fairies
Smelling the flowers
No bills to think of
No stress in the world
To be Peter Pan for one day
Play and be free
Creative juices flowing
Exploring the unknown
Nothing to think of
To be Peter Pan for one day
Playing with my friends
Eating fairy floss all day
Lying amongst the daffodils
Frolicking with the horses
Just to be Peter Pan for one day

Day 42 — Thoughts

To have my mum's arms around me
To keep me safe
To show me understanding
To whisper softly that everything will be all right
To hold on so tight that I'll have to fight to let go
A mother hen keeping guard
To reach out
A mother who is warm
Shines her brightness onto you
Smothering you with her heart
Pride in her eyes
Easing your burden
A mother who paves the way
How do I become that mother
When my shadow is so long
My heart yearns for what never was
Never could be
To be the mother I struggle to know
To bear my soul so that my shoulders aren't heavy
To be the mum I struggle to see
I want to be what I have longed for
A mother to hold her arms open for me

Day 43 — Australia

The Australian sun
Scorches all in its path
It is not for the gentle spirit
The beaches can be harsh if unprepared
The backyard is nowhere to be, under the Australian sun
A barbecue at sunset is a must
There is nowhere to hide
Walk barefoot I dare you
You've never walked so fast
The Australian sunburn is a baptism of fire
The hardiest of the natural life survives
The trees are our saviour
Days on end and no relief from the blistering heat
The heat slivers through your bedroom, unable to sleep
When will it rain
When will the winds change
When will the sun hide
The Australian sun is a blessing and a curse
We long for the sun
We wish for a reprieve from the sun
Be wary of the Australian sun

Day 44 — Fairy

How I want to be a fairy
Fly here fly there
Sprinkle a little fairy dust everywhere
Curl up in a flower bud
Be bright for all to see
Cast a magic spell
Play tricks on all who walk by
Sit high with the birds
Let the daffodils be my blanket
Oh to be a fairy
Tip toe tip toe, don't let anyone see
Mischievous deeds
Imagination runs rife
Play hide and seek with a mouse
To be so little and so bold
Nature by my side
To be a fairy would be nice

Day 45 — Storms

Thunder and lightning
Fireworks in the sky
The storms have come
The skies have settled
The air is fresh
Jump in the puddles left behind
The cool air breathes new life
The birds flit looking for a place to rest
The plants sigh with relief
The storm has not devastated us today
The storm has delivered us from the scorching sun
Breathe in breathe out
The storm will pass
We rejoice in the rain
It's time to go outside to play
No fear of the sun today
The sun has shied away for today

Day 46 — Protection

The desperation in her eyes
The helplessness in her heart
Sorrow springs forth
All she wants to do is protect her young
The young want to flee
They want to spread their wings
They don't understand the danger
The young want to run wild
They haven't seen the world for what it is
The tricksters around every corner
The protector can only do so much
The mother hen can only fight off so many wolves
Watch out for the clowns with sad faces
Heed the warnings young ones
Life can be a perilous journey
Be brave
Be aware
Never forget to reach out
Let your heart stay true
And wisdom guide your light
You have an angel in your corner

Day 47 — New

New job
New home
New experience
New relationship
Navigation of the new
The new people, don't talk too much
Don't show all your colours too quickly
Navigating the new
Anxiousness takes hold
How do I dress
What if the new is over my head
I don't want to offend
Navigating new experiences, can I do this
What are the expectations placed upon me
How do I make it easier
Navigate new ways
Navigate new meanings
My head is buzzing inside like a hive of bees
The responsibility is new
I don't know what I'm doing
All this new can be difficult to manage
The new will pass
The new will just be
The new creates resilience

The new enhances learning
The new builds strength
Don't be afraid of the new

Day 48 — Creepy Crawlies

Creepy crawlies
Snakes
Flies
Spiders that are deadly to their own
The predatory life down under
The mosquitoes at night time
Are you prepared
Are you aware what may crawl in your bed
The huntsman find a home near you to get their prey
The daddy long legs eat those that may cause you harm
Beware of the ants, some of them bite
The flies can leave a pinch
Are you ready to brave the outdoors
Snakes looking for shade, but don't cross their path
I don't like spiders
Do you
They exist by our side
Can you tell the friendly from the frightening
Who would be brave enough to live amongst this night life
Would you know what to do
Would you be brave
These creatures live close by
Never too far away
Are you brave enough to cross their path

Day 49 — Summer End

The end of summer is upon us
The breeze is cooler
The raindrops, hesitant
The animals scurry for shelter
Our bodies cool down
We long for those summer days again
Cooler days are refreshing for the spirit
Hot chocolate soothes the soul
Blankets provide comfort
The mornings are darker
Dragging oneself out of bed is difficult in the cool air
Warming by the fire is what eases our bodies
Comfort foods of childhoods gone by
Pets snuggle close to take your warmth
Fresh air keeps us alert
The cool air has started its journey
We are bound by the change until the sun greets us again

Day 50 — Restlessness

Another sleepless night
Another midnight bath
Hopefully I have the right concoction this time
A bit of this a bit of that and I'll feel sleepy
Will the pain dissipate even if it's temporary
We will have to wait and see
I have to get up early
How will I manage through the day
Daydreaming my way through, losing focus
Wake up I tell myself
Only a few more hours and I can go back to bed
Working a necessary evil
Stimulates mental activity, but creates havoc on the weary
The pain is close to unbearable
The darkness starts to set in
What if I cut myself to divert the pain
If I don't wake up will I be in a better place
The bath concoction does not seem to be settling me
More pills just to gain a few hours' sleep
Why is that the only answer
My skin is on fire
The pain is relentless
I'm being attacked by my own system

The control pad is not working any more
Something sinister has control
I'm out of answers
Minute by minute
Hour by hour
Day by day
This is how I will overcome the darkness
The pain
Cling to my comforts
Dwell in positive moments
This is how my life is

www.ingramcontent.com/pod-product-compliance
Lightning Source LLC
LaVergne TN
LVHW041543060526
838200LV00037B/1118